In this guide to grooming horses, Jo
Cindy Weaver show you the secrets
that contribute to their success.

MW00824390

Clipping

This information originally appeared in Western Horseman Magazine *as a 5-part series, July-November 1994. Because of its popularity, we've reproduced it in this booklet.*

—*Kathy Kadash*
Associate Editor

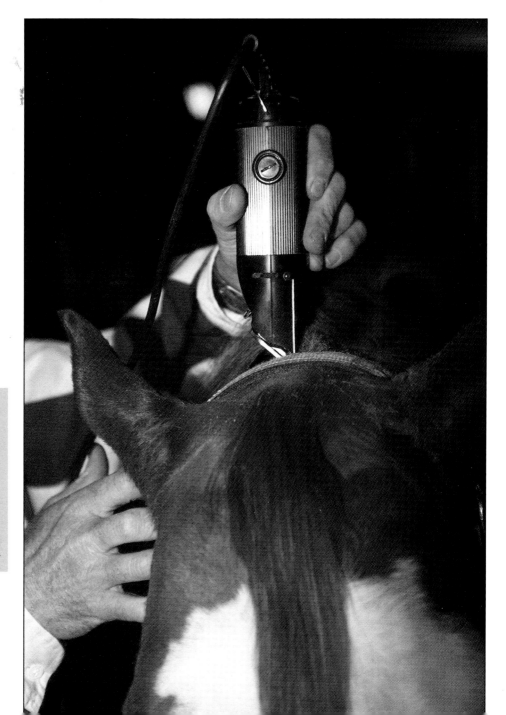

*C*lipping is an art. If you don't know what you're doing, you can really do a bad job. It doesn't matter if you need the closeness of a show clip with cleaned-out ears and a whiskerless muzzle or want the practicality of simply getting rid of leg feather and having a bridle path. There are successful techniques to master, and it takes a little practice to get good at not scalping your horse.

Trainers John and Cindy Weaver take special pride in their abilities to turn out good-looking, well-groomed show horses. When it comes to grooming, they each have their specialties. John is the artist with clipper blades and Cindy is the expert at mane and tail care. In this first part on clipping, John shows you how he clips a horse from the leg up.

Pre-Clipping

The day before he clips, John washes the horse's legs, or at least rinses them to remove dust and dirt. Clipper blades last a lot longer if they don't have to clip through dirt and grime.

"And I do a much better job of clipping if the hair is clean," says John, "because I get a much more consistent flow to the blade. Then, just before I clip, I brush off the legs once more to remove any light dust, dirt, shavings, etc."

Best Time to Clip

John likes to clip in the evening, when it's a lot quieter around the barn. Also, at that time the horses have finished eating, so they're full

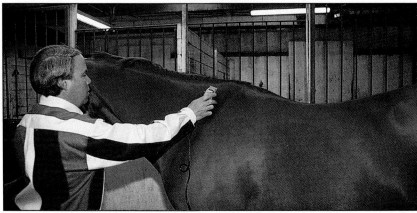

To familiarize the horse with the hum and vibration of the clippers, John first massages the horse's body with quiet ear clippers.

and settled. The middle of the day can be hectic, with other horses milling around and going by. The horse you're clipping can become too distracted to stand still and give you his full attention.

Preventing Problems

When John gets a horse (young or old) who hasn't been clipped before, or even one who hasn't been clipped for a long time, he gives the horse a chance to get used to the procedure first. He doesn't just start clipping. Instead, he uses a massage technique that has helped him immeasurably over the years in preventing problems.

First, he holds the horse with a lead rope; he doesn't put him in cross-ties. A scared horse in cross-ties could hurt himself and anyone around him if he lunges forward or back. John uses his quietest set of ear clippers because they aren't as strong or loud, and don't vibrate as much as body clippers. He touches the horse's body all over with the clippers, starting at the withers and going over the back. This helps the horse get used to the hum and vibration of the clippers, and they don't seem so threatening to the horse. He doesn't put the clippers, even quiet ones, up near the horse's face or ears at this point. That might cause the horse to

Profile

John and Cindy Weaver are a highly successful and versatile husband-wife team. They both are capable of showing at halter, and then turning right around and riding in performance classes. They own and operate a breeding, training, and showing facility, catering to Paint and Quarter Horses.

John and Cindy make their living by producing and presenting both halter and performance horses (specializing in western pleasure and hunter under saddle) and they have a solid youth and amateur program. In Paint Horse competition through 1992, the Weavers have produced 12 world or national champions, 11 APHA champions, 25 top 10 honor roll titles, and over 75 Superior Horse awards. In 1993 they added eight more APHA national and top 10 honor roll awards, including the number one 13-and-under showmanship exhibitor, the fourth place all-age western pleasure horse, and the reserve world champion junior mare. They have recently included Quarter Horses in their show program.

Weaver Training Center is located at 2144 S. I-25, Castle Rock, CO 80104; 303-688-5530.

become apprehensive immediately.

I touch the horse with the body of the clippers, not the actual blades," explains John. "I rub the horse all over. He gets used to the noise and realizes it's not a fly or mosquito."

Only after he is satisfied that the horse accepts the noise and vibration on his body does John work down the legs with the body of the clippers. Again, by just touching the horse with the clipper body, if the horse does kick, he won't kick the clipper blades or catch the point of the clipper and nick his skin.

When John is through, he puts the horse back into his stall. He doesn't clip him that day. He may use the same massage techniques for days, depending on the mental state of the horse.

This seems to help horses overcome their nervousness about being clipped. "I like to eliminate traumatic experiences," John says. "That's better for the horse and me."

Clippers

John uses two sets of clippers for different parts of the horse's body. One is a lightweight, adjustable ear clipper. On the side of the clipper, an adjustment lever lets you alter the blade closeness from surgical all the way to a coarse clip.

The other type is a heavier, body clipper with removable blades, with each having a different strength or closeness. The difference between the two has to do with vibration and movement of the blades. The ear clipper blades are made to clip downward (with the grain) and the body clippers are made to clip upward (against the grain). John has extra sets in case one breaks.

"I keep all my clippers, blades, and any necessary items, such as twitches, lubricating sprays, and ointments, in a tackle box," John states. "That reduces the amount of dust and dirt that gets into the clippers, which can ruin them. I service my clippers a couple times a year and my blades get sharpened a lot. I always keep an extra set of blades in case I drop them or they get dull. It's just like anything else. You have to keep your tools in proper order when you don't need them because the minute you do need them, that's when you'll find out they're not working. So it's important to keep everything neat and clean."

Blades

Blades are categorized by numbers—10, 15, 30, 40—and the numbers refer to degrees of closeness in the shave they give. Generally, a 10

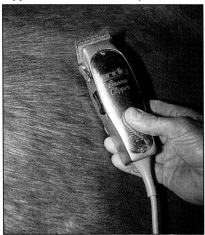

The lever on the side of this adjustable ear clipper alters the closeness of the blades.

blade gives the coarsest cut and a 40 the closest. The latter is called a surgical blade because it cuts down to the skin line. If you have a 40 blade and clip against the grain of the hair, you will get a lot closer to the skin. However, in the case of white leg and face markings, you'll have pink skin showing.

With solid colored legs and faces, the hair will be of a lighter shade than the surrounding hair coat and that isn't attractive, either. If you don't want either the pink-skin look or lighter colored hair, then clip with the grain of the hair.

Blades have differing numbers of teeth. On a coarse-haired horse or one who has long hair, John likes to use the standard, wide, 18-tooth blade because it goes through the hair faster. However, it leaves clipper marks or tracks. On a horse with a slick, summer coat, he uses a 22-tooth blade. The finer blades make it look as if the clipped area hadn't been shaved at all.

Body

In this article, we'll concentrate on clipping only the face and legs of the horse, not the entire body.

The coats of horses who must be body-clipped do not reflect their true color. For example, a chestnut horse might have an orange-colored coat and a bay will look light brown. Also, the hair coat is usually dry. If John absolutely must body clip, he keeps the horse on special vitamin supplements for 30 days prior to clipping. Then, when he clips, the skin and hair still look oily, not dry.

However, 95 percent of the time, he would prefer not to clip the entire body. "If you body clip in the North, the coat gets out of seasonal sequence and might be off for about a year," he explains. For example, a horse clipped in late fall might begin growing a winter coat the following spring.

"You also have to give the horse a lot of hot oil baths and use double blankets to keep him warm. I would rather spend the 90 days it takes to get a horse ready naturally, because it takes that long to get the horse's body toned up anyway."

Legs

When clipping legs, John usually puts horses in cross-ties, provided they're good about being clipped. If not, a helper holds the lead rope as John works.

John starts clipping the legs first

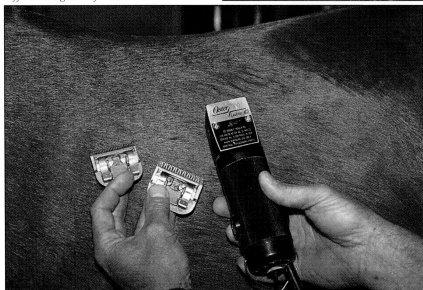

The removable blades on this clipper have different degrees of closeness.

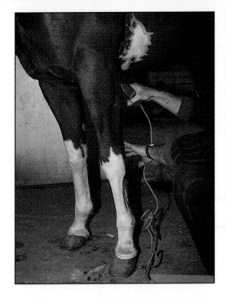

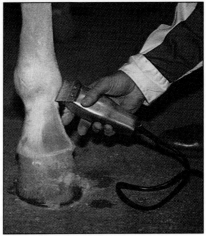

With the adjustable ear clipper, John feathers all the way down the leg, from the forearm to the coronet band.

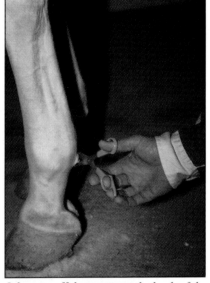

John cuts off the ergots on the back of the fetlocks with a pair of scissors.

To clip the crevices of the cannon bones, John pulls or stretches the skin one way and then the other to make it easier to clip.

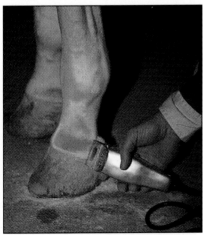

Finishing off the coronet band with a close shave.

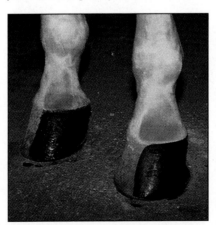

The difference between shaving the coronet band closely and not shaving it can really be seen after applying hoof black. On the shaved leg on the right, the line made by the hoof black is clean and neat. On the unshaved coronet band on the left, the hoof black line is ragged.

because it helps to calm the horse. If a horse has a problem with clipping, it's generally with the head. Even with a horse who has been regularly clipped for years, John still starts with the legs. "I think it lets a horse knows what's coming, and it doesn't scare him."

John prefers not to boot a horse, a common practice in which the horse is clipped from the coronet band up to the knee. After booting, it takes awhile for the hair to grow in, maybe a week.

"Since I like to clip a day or so before a show, I don't have the time to wait for hair to grow," he explains.

Instead, with an adjustable ear clipper, he feathers all the way down the leg with different blades and degrees of pressure. Feathering means he uses light, long, even strokes. A lot depends on how much hair the horse has. He doesn't want the horse to look scalped. "I may use a 15 blade from the shoulder down to just above the knee, and then I'll go to a 30 from the knee down to the pastern, then a 40 blade from there down to the coronet band."

For thick, heavy, leg feathers, such as those found on a winter or early spring hair coat, he uses a 15 or 30 blade on the body clippers.

"I don't care what the hair looks like at first," he states. "The stronger blades will go through that long hair. I get down to a quarter of an inch of workable hair. If I tried to use fine-tooth clippers on a horse who just came in from the pasture with real

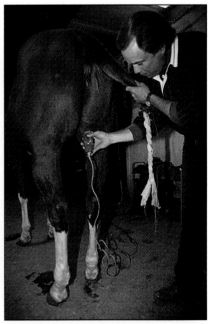

As a finishing touch, John clips the hair between the hind legs.

long hair, the blades wouldn't go through it. So, first I remove the real long hair, and then use the finer blades for close grooming."

He first clips from the top of the forearm to the knee; there's a natural breaking point just above the knee joint where he stops. He clips all the way around the forearm of the leg. Horses have chestnuts on the inside of their forearms and John peels them off with his fingers. Then, he clips closely around them. If he peeled off the chestnut after he clipped, he'd still have some long hair around it. Generally, fingernails are all you need to pick off a chestnut; but if you have a large one that gives you trouble, John suggests using a pair of scissors to clip off the top part. That will get you started and peeling should be easier after that.

After clipping the forearm, John takes the blade down to a 30 (moves the adjustable lever to the 30 slot, which makes the cut finer) and clips from the knee and cannon bone down to fetlock and then to the coronet band.

To clip in the crevices of the tendons on the cannon bones, he pulls the skin with his fingers and rolls it out of the crevices, first one way and then the other to clip the entire area.

Horses have an ergot on the back of their fetlocks. John twists off the ergot or cuts it off with scissors, which allows him to clip closely around the area without the ergot getting in the way.

The final step in clipping the leg is finishing off the coronet band. With the blade in the 40 position on the ear clippers, John clips along the coronet band, above the hoof. This close shave helps when he puts on hoof black because it prevents the liquid hoof polish from running up the hair. By doing this, he can make a nice, neat line with the hoof black around the top of the hoof. If he didn't, the line between the hoof and the coronet band could get shabby-looking.

Head

When he clips the horse's head, John doesn't cross-tie in case the animal becomes scared. Cross-tied horses who become frightened can be seriously injured. Either a helper holds the lead rope, or John drapes it over an arm.

He usually starts at the tip of the nose and works up to the ears. "I do the things the horse tolerates best

From the Inside Out

If there is one thing that John and Cindy Weaver stress, it's that all the grooming, bathing, and clipping in the world won't help a horse who isn't healthy from the inside out. There isn't a shampoo on the market that can make a wormy horse look healthy, and not even the best clip job can make a thin horse appear to be in good condition. If the horse isn't ready physically, grooming won't help.

Here's a health program the Weavers recommend:

1/ De-worming — It's imperative that the horse be on a regular de-worming program. The Weavers tube-worm every 30 to 60 days. The weanlings and yearlings are on a 30-day schedule. After that age, they go on a 60- to 90-day schedule. After years of trying both the tubing and pasting methods of de-worming, the Weavers have found that tube-worming gives their horses better hair coats than paste worming.

2/ Dental — Teeth are checked every 6 months and floated if necessary. Having the teeth in good shape helps a horse obtain maximum benefit from his hay and grain.

3/ Farrier — A regular program helps eliminate a lot of soundness and foot care problems. Even in the winter, when horses' hoofs don't seem to grow as much or as fast, John and Cindy maintain regular trimming and shoeing schedules. They don't think you can solve a problem that's been brewing for 3 or 4 months after only one shoeing in the spring.

4/ Nutrition — The Weavers feed each horse individually. Some have a higher metabolism and are therefore more energetic. Some are lethargic or laid back. All of their horses (halter and riding) are not on the same feed program. The amounts vary with the horse. Some you can push a little harder; some you can't.

They watch each horse carefully and change feed as needed. If the feed needs to be increased or decreased, they do it gradually. They warn that you shouldn't double the feed ration and protein levels all of a sudden on a horse who needs just a little bit of weight, or immediately cut in half the ration of a horse who needs to lose weight. This is especially true for a halter horse you want to start riding. You can't simply cut his ration and protein level in half. It takes awhile to get his mind right. A horse on a high grain ration and protein level is usually full of energy, making him harder to ride. And it also takes time to shape a different kind of muscle.

If the Weavers had to put their health program in one word, it would be consistency. "You must have consistent vet work, consistent farrier work, consistent feed, consistent exercise. "The whole thing wraps around consistency," John insists. "That's how you have the ultimate effect on a horse. If the horse is potentially a 9, then to make him a full 9 you have to approach him with a consistent program. If you have a 7, you probably can't make him into a 10, but you can improve him to a point. To make the horse the best he can be, you need a consistent program. If you don't have that consistency, you won't be as competitive as you could be."

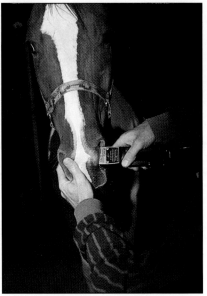

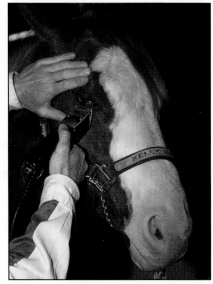

To clip the face, John first trims around the lips and under the chin.

John clips lightly inside the nostrils.

John is especially careful around the eyes, but the long lashes under the lower lids must be trimmed as closely as possible.

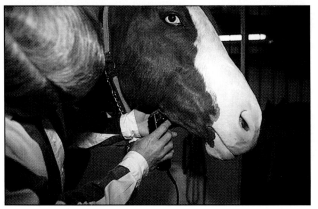

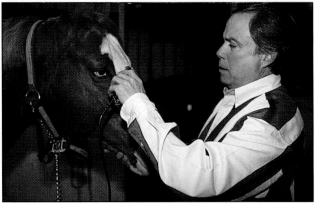

To make it easier to clip the face and jaw, John removes the horse's halter. First, he clips under the jaw.

Then he feathers from the center of the nasal bone all the way around to the bottom of the jaw with long, smooth strokes.

first, such as the lips and nose, and work my way up to the ears."

John uses body clippers for the face. Unless a horse has just come in from pasture and has really long hair on his face, most of the face work is done with 30 and 40 blades. In the summertime when the horse is really slick, he uses a 40 over the entire head.

Here's how to clip more specific parts of the head.

Nose and Muzzle

John starts with a 40 blade on the nose and keeps a 30 blade in his back pocket so it's easy to change blades.

He clips around the lips, under the chin, around the nostrils, and very lightly inside the nostrils, both front and back. "A lot of horses aren't receptive to this when you start," John states, "but if you go slowly and try not to catch the horse's skin, they eventually realize it's not going to hurt them. Then they tolerate it."

John suggests not going too far inside the nostril and losing sight of the clipper blade, but you can get the edges of the nostrils.

"In the beginning, I take a clipper that's not on and rub the blade around and inside the nose, just like I did in massaging the horse's body. That helps the horse get used to the feeling that something is in his nose before the vibration starts."

Eye

Continuing with the 40 blade, John clips around the eye, upper and lower lid, being careful not to get the eyelashes on the upper lid. The long lashes under the lower lid have to be trimmed as closely as possible without injuring the eye.

Face and Jaw

For this part of the head, John takes off the halter and fastens it around the horse's neck so he has a totally unobstructed area to clip. However, if you are clipping a young

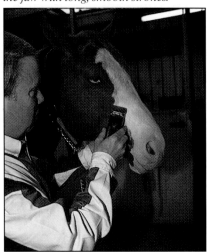

horse or one who isn't familiar with this procedure, then loosen the halter enough to be able to get the clippers between the halter and the chin. You'll still have a good hold on the horse.

"It's amazing how quickly horses will respond," he says, "and you'll be able to clip easily, especially if you

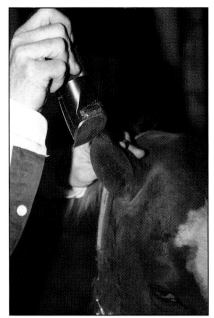

Clipping the outside of the ear . . .

support the horse's head with your free hand."

John takes the 40 blade and clips from the bottom of the horse's jaw down to the chin. Then he takes a 30 blade and feathers from the center of the nasal bone all the way around to the bottom of the jaw with long, smooth strokes.

Ears

When clipping the head, John does the ears last, since they are the most sensitive part of a horse. That's usually where you'll have a problem and when you'll have to twitch the horse. If you start with the ears and then do the rest of face, the horse might be upset from having his ears done and then not stand still while the rest of the face or even the legs are being clipped.

If this is the horse's first clip of the season, John does the outside of the ears with either a 15 or 30 blade, and a 30 or 40 on the inside. After a horse has been clipped a few times, the hair is already short; so he uses a 30 blade on the outside and a 40 on the inside.

When clipping the ears, John twitches all his horses because that usually ensures they don't move. The horse gets a nice, even clip job inside his ear. Also, the twitch helps protect the horse, especially when John is using a sharp 40 blade inside an ear. The horse's movement can cause the person doing the clipping to slip and the blade might nick the horse's ear. Then, in the future, the horse will be less likely to let you clip his ears.

If the horse still fights getting his ears done, the Weavers have a set of

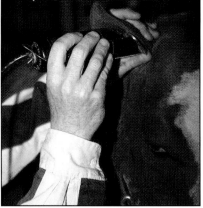

. . . then the inside.

John removes some tufts of hair at the base of the ear.

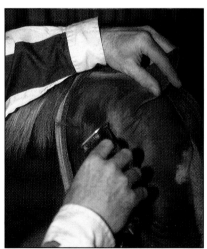

The long hair on either side of the ear is trimmed.

stocks that limits the horse's movement. However, most people aren't fortunate to have stocks at home. In that case, John suggests confining the horse—putting him in his stall and snubbing him to something sturdy. Then twitch the horse and try again.

When clipping a foal, John usually starts by going around the ears with the clippers, just barely touching a little hair. Then he comes back a week

Handy Hint #1

John always starts clipping with a brand new or re-sharpened set of blades. The instant he feels a little pull on the hair, he knows the blades are not cutting as cleanly as they did, and he changes them immediately.

To keep blades clean and cool during clipping, John uses blade wash on the blades he uses to clip the legs, and a lubricating spray on the blades he uses to clip the face.

John suggests checking the temperature of the blades every few minutes during clipping. By placing them on the back of your hand, you can tell what they feel like to the horse. If the blade get warm, stop clipping, and use blade wash or coolant to cool and clean the blades. They help reduce friction on the blades, and, therefore, reduce heat. Some of today's clippers, however, can run a long while without getting hot.

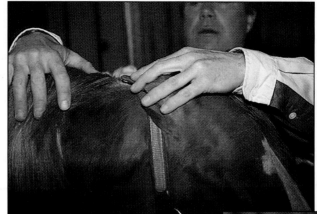

Handy Hint #2

If a horse is not a show horse, there is no reason to clip out the hair from inside the ears. In the summer, the hair will protect the horse from flies and gnats and, in the winter, it will give some protection from the cold. Show horses need their ears clipped, but even then, the length of hair in the ear depends on the time of year and what they're shown in.

later and does it again. "I gradually get the foal used to the sensation. When it comes to ears, I'm a lot slower with young horses. If I take my time when the horse is young, he is better as an older horse. If you scare one early on, he may always have a problem with his ears."

Bridle Path

After the ears, John does the bridle path, using a 40 blade.

There is a rule of thumb regarding the length of a bridle path that John and other pros follow. Take the horse's ear and gently bend it back toward the mane. The point where the tip of the ear touches the horse is the farthest point back where you should clip the bridle path. This rule does not necessarily apply to Arabians and other breeds that are presented with longer bridle paths, often extending up to 8 or more inches.

Horses with really thick throat-latches sometimes benefit from longer

The bridle path should be no farther forward than the point of the poll.

bridle paths. It's an optical illusion and makes the horse with a thick throat-latch look slimmer in that area and longer in the neck.

The bridle path should begin no farther forward than the point where the poll starts to drop on the horse's forehead. There is a prominent knob that you can feel easily with your fingers.

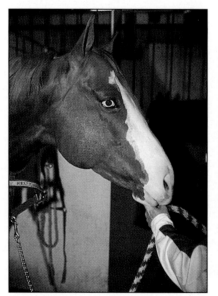

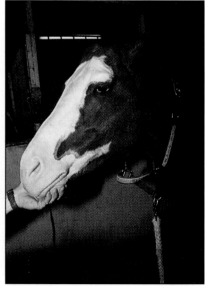

The finished product. Compare the right or clipped side of the horse's head to the left or unclipped side.

A well-groomed horse is a clean
one. Cindy Weaver shows you
how to get the job done.

Bathing

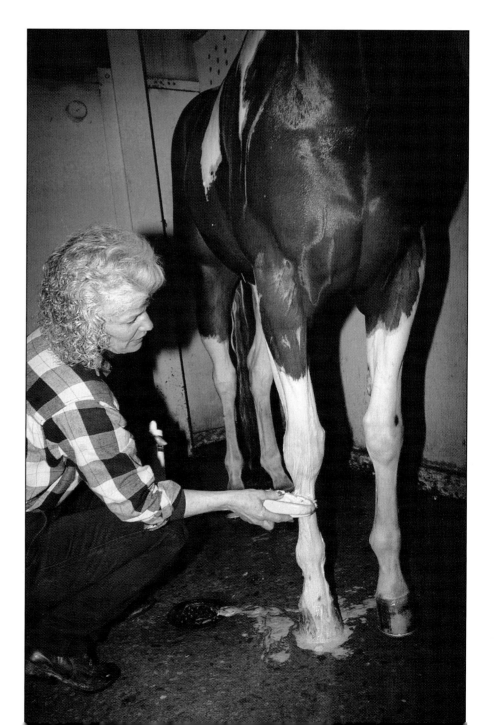

C indy shows you how she washes a horse and how to handle those tough yellow stains.

Wash area

Weaver Training Center has a wash rack with hot and cold water, but any area that drains well will work. You can certainly bathe a horse outside, providing the weather is warm and you have a good stout post or tree for tying the horse.

When washing a horse used to getting baths, Cindy usually puts the horse in cross-ties in the wash rack. But with younger horses, such as weanlings, or horses who have not had a lot of experience getting baths in confined areas, Cindy has someone hold the animal for the first several times. When the horse is comfortable with everything, she washes him without help and just ties the horse to a single rope on the wash rack wall. In time, and only after she feels the horse is confident about getting a bath, Cindy uses the cross-ties to secure the horse.

"I find cross-ties can panic a young horse, and I don't want to do that," says Cindy. "I want to make washing a pleasant experience, especially because we're usually working with show horses and they have to be washed so much in their lives."

Rinse

Cindy rinses the horse's entire body with warm water, which horses tolerate better than cold. How she rinses depends on the horse. For a horse experienced with bathing, she starts with the neck and works down the body, leaving the face for last. But for a younger horse or one who is not used to baths, she starts with the front legs and works up the body slowly. She doesn't move to the rest of the body until the horse is quiet about having his legs hosed.

Next, she goes to the shoulder area and works backward across the back to the croup and down the hind legs. If the horse gets nervous at any time, she goes back to the front legs and works up again until the horse is quiet.

On an inexperienced horse, she leaves the neck until last, since such a horse can get nervous about water being sprayed around his head.

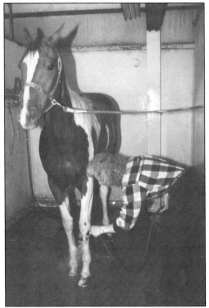
When washing a young horse or one who isn't used to getting a bath, Cindy starts rinsing the lower legs first to accustom the horse to the spray.

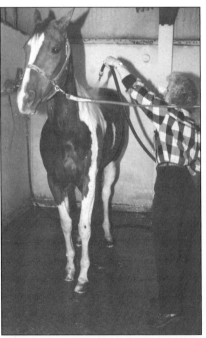
Cindy always points the spray nozzle toward the back of the horse.

When it comes to rinsing, Cindy doesn't rinse and wash one side at a time. "If you do," she explains. "you've just distributed the dirt from one side to the other. So I rinse both sides first, then scrub all over, then rinse off both sides again."

After she has rinsed the entire body, Cindy soaks the mane and tail thoroughly. Then she applies shampoo.

When she sprays or rinses the horse, Cindy always points the nozzle of the hose toward the back of the horse, so she is always washing the dirt or suds to the back and down the horse. Also, by pointing the hose toward the back, there isn't as much chance of getting the water in the horse's ears.

Washing

Cindy likes to use a hard-bristle brush, rather than a sponge, because she feels the brush brings up dead hair better. However, she will use a sponge on a sensitive horse. Her favorite wash brush is small, fits right in the palm of her hand, and has a handle for a secure grip. With this type of brush she can work up a good scrubbing motion.

Since Cindy and John have many Paint show horses in their barn, dealing with dirty and stained white markings and manes and tails is a continual problem. They rely on one of the whitening shampoos on the market, designed specifically for getting out stains on horses. Most tack stores have these products in their grooming sections. They are called whiteners or bluing agents, although the shampoo is purple.

After the horse is rinsed and before the actual soap scrubbing, Cindy puts the purple whitening shampoo on her brush and scrubs it on the stained white areas of the body, legs, mane, and tail. She lets it set while she scrubs the rest of the horse with regular shampoo. Given some time, the whitening agent does its magic on the stain. One note of caution, however. Don't let the purple shampoo set more than 15 minutes, or the horse's hair will have a purple stain, or at the least, purple highlights.

When the horse is wet, the yellow stain may still look a little bit yellow, Cindy says. But as the horse dries, the yellow will turn white. Sometimes,

Cindy prefers to apply a small amount of soap to the brush.

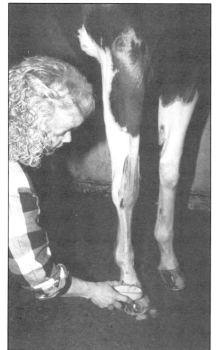

Purple whitening shampoo should stay on the horse's body for no longer than 15 minutes, or else it will leave a stain. Notice that Cindy also scrubs the horse's hoofs.

Many horses dislike having their faces washed. Cindy works on getting the horse's confidence so she can get it done.

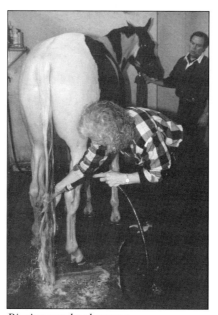

Rinsing out the shampoo.

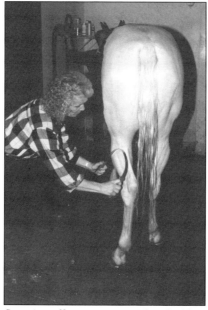

Scraping off excess water with a shedding blade.

there will be a gray cast to the area, but that usually is not apparent in the show ring.

The whitener may not be able to remove extremely bad yellow stains the first time it is applied. It may have to be used two or three times before the stains disappear. For some white tails that have been neglected for a long time, it may take a month of continually using the whitener to get any noticeable results. White tails, especially on show horses, need to be kept in a tail sack or bag to keep them clean.

For everyday washing, Cindy uses one of the many shampoos on the market. For show days, she prefers to use one of the shampoos that contains a sheen ingredient (extra shine, highlights, etc.).

For scrubbing, Cindy puts the soap on the brush and some on the horse's body. "I don't like to over-soap a horse," Cindy explains. "I think a lot of people feel the more suds they see, the cleaner the horse is going to be. But I find that it takes a lot of rinsing to get some of the soaps out, especially the more concentrated ones. So I try not to use an excessive amount of soap. I also don't use a bucket with soap in the water. I find it much easier to soap the brush or the horse. And I don't drip soap all over the horse. I just use a little dot on my brush or that part of the body I am going to do."

Cindy also scrubs the horse's hoofs. That makes it easier to apply hoof black or some sort of a hoof dressing.

Cindy leaves the horse's face for last, after the horse is quiet and relaxed from the rest of the bath. For the face, she uses a wider, softer water spray than she used in bathing the horse's body. With one hand, she holds the horse's head by the halter; and with the nozzle in the other hand, she slowly and carefully brings the hose up to the horse's face and aims the spray at the horse's forehead, right between his eyes. Once the horse gets used to that, she carefully aims the spray nozzle around the face, being careful to avoid getting the water in the ears and eyes.

To wash the face, Cindy uses the same brush she used in scrubbing the horse's body; and as before, she puts a small amount of soap on the brush. She scrubs gently, only applying as much pressure as the horse will stand. Once the face is clean, she rinses it off in the same manner she used to get it wet.

As for the ears, most horses turn them backward when being sprayed with water. That helps prevent water from running into them. And, too, since Cindy is using a gentle spray on the forehead between the eyes and ears, the water drips downward and not into the ears. The ears do not need to be soaped or rinsed. Cindy uses the damp chamois or cloth to wipe them, inside and out.

Washing and rinsing around the eyes requires some common sense. Cindy is careful about the aim of the spray, and she only uses shampoo that is of the non-sting variety. It's never necessary to spray directly into the eye socket.

For a horse who just won't tolerate water sprayed on his face, Cindy uses a sponge or chamois to get the job done.

"I use warm water for the face, as I do the rest of the body," says Cindy, "and horses don't seem to mind it as much as they do cold water. I try to have my horses' heads washed at home before we get to the shows, where many times only cold water is available."

After she washes the horse, Cindy rinses him in the same manner she did when she started.

Conditioner

After the body scrubbing and rinse, Cindy works a conditioner into the mane and the tail with a large, wide-tooth comb.

"I'm careful not to snag the hair," she explains. "I pick the snag or tangled hair out or work through it carefully with the wide-tooth comb until the hair falls free. Sometimes, if a tail is extremely tangled, I just keep working the hair with water, then conditioner, then more water, followed by more conditioner, until I can pick the tangles out. I don't use a brush on tails when they are wet, because that would have a tendency to pull out the hair. After I get the tangles out, I can run through the hair with a regular-sized comb."

Cindy says to make sure the conditioning products you put on manes and tails aren't oil-based. Oil collects dust and grime, making it difficult to comb through the mane and tail easily.

Many of the conditioners are designed to be left in the mane and tail and don't need to be rinsed out. However, it also doesn't hurt to do so.

Shedding water

Cindy scrapes off excess water by using the smooth side of a typical shedding blade, not the side that has teeth for pulling out winter hair. She runs the blade over the horse's body, but not down the legs. For the legs, she uses a cloth that absorbs liquid, similar to a chamois, or, she says, you could even use a chamois.

With the chamois in both hands, she runs down the legs, squeezing the water into it. That helps dry the leg quickly. A dry leg doesn't attract as much dirt as a wet leg. Cindy frequently wrings out the chamois or cloth between legs, because it does absorb water.

Sheen

The many sheen products on the market are excellent for helping to keep a horse clean after a bath. They help repel dirt and yellow stains and are great for untangling manes and

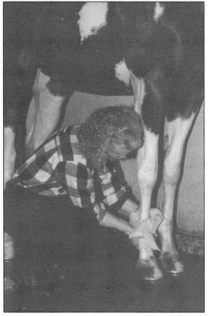

A chamois squeezes water off the horse's legs.

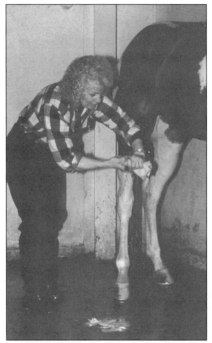

Cindy wrings out a waterlogged chamois.

tails. They are sprayed on and left.

After she rinses the horse thoroughly and has removed any excess water from the body and legs, Cindy applies a sheen product all over the horse. However, on performance horses, she doesn't spray sheen where the saddle goes because that can make the saddle slip. Halter horses, on the other hand, get sheen all over.

For forelocks, Cindy sprays sheen into her hand and rubs it into the forelock. She never sprays the sheen directly on the horse's face.

After the bath

Once the horse is washed, Cindy

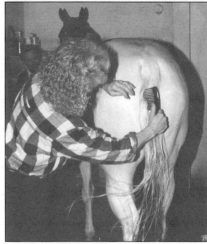

A large, wide-toothed comb helps untangle knots in a tail.

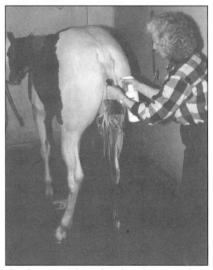

Cindy sprays the tail with a sheen product.

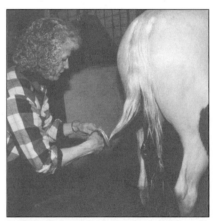

Before she puts the horse back in his stall, Cindy ties several simple knots in the tail to lift it off the ground.

returns him to his stall and ties him up, so he doesn't roll. If he has a long tail that drags the ground, she ties several simple knots in it to raise the hair off the ground. Once the horse's body is partially dry, she puts on a light sheet and unties the horse. Then, the tail is braided or put into a tail bag or sack, until show time.

When it comes to manes,
the horses under John and Cindy Weaver's care
never have a bad hair day.

Mane Care

Before and after shots. The photo on the left shows a fairly long and thick mane. The photo on the right shows it pulled, thinned, banded, and ready for the show ring.

ONE OF THE MOST noticeable things about a well-groomed horse, besides the condition of his coat, is the condition of his mane. Thick, unruly, uneven, and rubbed-out manes are unsightly and don't say much about the care an owner gives his horse.

John and Cindy show how they prepare manes for the show ring. Whether you show your horse or not, the Weavers' tips can help you solve some of the problems you may be having with your horse's mane.

Before You Get Started

For pulling and thinning, John and Cindy like a mane that hasn't been washed or conditioned, since that makes the hair too fluffy and slippery to work with. Dirt and grime on the hair shafts actually make the pulling and thinning process easier.

As for the length of time it takes to pull and thin a mane, a lot depends on the amount of hair a horse has and his tolerance level.

"On a horse with a long, thick mane, it might take several sessions to get it as thin as you want," explains John. "The horse's patience or tolerance level plays a part. Most horses don't care to have their manes pulled, so you usually have to do a little bit at a time."

Pulling hair out by the roots does smart a little. With a really thin mane, you won't have to pull at all. Just use thinning shears to keep the ends trimmed on a weekly or bimonthly basis. Thinning doesn't bother a horse.

About mane care in general, John says it's difficult to explain thoroughly because it's like cutting hair. It's hard to tell someone how to cut someone else's hair. "The experience of doing it over and over again will make it easier," John says. In this case, as in all things, practice makes perfect. For example, John says: "Once you get

used to banding manes, the whole procedure will probably take you 10 to 15 minutes. But when you first start, it might take you 20 to 30 minutes. So don't be alarmed at the time it takes. The more you do it, the more proficient you'll become."

Equipment

Here are the items John and Cindy use to pull and thin a mane.

1/ A metal pulling comb. A small comb with short teeth that are close together. Cindy likes the kind with a handle at one end, but pulling combs do come without handles. (Can be found in tack stores.)

2/ Thinning shears. These are scissors with short, unevenly spaced teeth. Unlike regular scissors, which make a

The tools of the trade (from left to right): pulling comb, alligator clip, bands, thinning shears, all on a step stool.

blunt cut, thinning shears cut every other hair in an uneven pattern. Once Cindy has the mane the length she wants, John uses thinning shears to thin the mane. (Can be found in tack stores.)

3/ Alligator clip. Big plastic comb with teeth that helps separate hairs of the mane while it is being banded. (Can be found at any discount store in hair care department.)

4/ Bands. Small rubber bands for banding short manes to make them lie flat. They come in two sizes and Cindy prefers to use the smaller bands because the big ones have to be wrapped too many times.

Bands come in four basic colors: black, white, gray, and reddish-brown. Some bands come in other colors, but Cindy doesn't think they look as good in manes as the four basic colors. She prefers to use bands that are close to the same color as the mane. "Some people like to use light-colored or white bands on dark manes. However, if you don't have a perfect banding job or if the horse has a less than perfect neckline, the bands are really going to be conspicuous."

On a flaxen mane, or one with variegated red and blond hairs, you have a choice of using reddish-brown or white bands.

Banding by hand isn't the only way

to get the job done. John noted that there are several banding aids or devices on the market that help speed up the procedure. (Bands and banding devices can be found in tack stores.)

5/ Step stool. The Weavers suggest using a step caddy or step stool, or even standing on a bucket, to work with a mane. You need to stand on something to get your arms level with the top of the horse's mane. (Can be found in department or discount stores.)

Length

Manes are usually trimmed to 2½ to 3 inches long. For pulling and thinning, Cindy prefers to work with a mane that hasn't been washed.

Approximately 2½ to 3 inches is the general rule of thumb for most manes on Quarter Horses, Paint Horses, and Appaloosas.

John uses the neck muscle as a guideline. There's a large neck muscle just below the crest of the mane. John likes to trim along a line created by that muscle as it travels the length of the neck. "I like manes on the shorter and thinner side because I think it makes the neck look more attractive," says John. "Also, when you're riding a horse, a short banded mane moves very little when you're loping or trotting down the rail. It creates a pretty picture. A longer mane tends to wave or bounce with each stride."

Pulling

To pull the mane, take a small section of hair and backcomb it with the pulling comb. (Ratting is another common term for backcombing.) Cindy advises backcombing only small sections of hair (10 to 15 strands), because the horse objects less to a few hairs being pulled out than to many at one time.

To backcomb, hold the strands of hair between two fingers of one hand; then take the comb in the other hand and move the teeth upward from the tips of the hair to the roots. This produces a rat's nest in the mane. Out of the small section of hair you originally took, you should have a few strands left that did not get ratted. Wrap those

To backcomb, Cindy takes a small section of hair and moves the teeth of the pulling comb upward from the tips of the hair to the roots.

Another term for backcombing is ratting, and this picture shows why. The backcombed hair forms what looks like a rat's nest.

After Cindy has ratted the section, a few strands of hair will remain in her hand. These are the strands she will try to pull out.

She wraps the strands of hair around the comb and pulls. This method saves wear and tear on her hands.

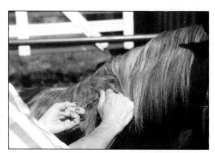

Another way of pulling is to hold the comb snug against the horse's neck and ratted mane, wrap the strands around fingers, and pull. This method can leave fingers sore and bruised after a while. Many people use a combination of both pulling methods.

After Cindy has gone through and ratted and pulled the mane a couple of times, it will start to shorten. However, there will be long hairs here and there. This gives her a guide where to pull.

strands of hair around the pulling comb as close to the roots of the mane as you can and pull downward. On a really long, thick mane, pulling close to the roots can be hard to do. The shorter the mane gets, the easier it is to pull close to the roots. As soon as you're through pulling the strand, comb through that section of hair. This often pulls out more hair. The procedure is four steps: backcomb, wrap, pull, and comb out.

"When pulling the mane, don't concentrate on just the outer layer of hair that you see," John explains. "It's important to pull the underneath hairs, as well. The mane's thickness varies from the top near the poll to the bottom near the withers. Obviously, you'll need to work longer on the thicker portions of the mane than the thinner ones."

Cindy adds: "You have to feel for thickness at the top of the mane, along the crest, because that is where you'll have to band."

Once the mane starts to shorten, Cindy says, you'll see edges of the mane that are still a little long. This gives you a guide and lets you know where you'll have to continue pulling to shorten.

Horses who won't allow their manes to be pulled can be a problem. John advises: "If you have a horse who is tolerant to having his mane pulled,

you can put him in cross-ties or simply tie him up. But there may be some cases when a horse will not stand still, and we put him in stocks. Occasionally, you may have to twitch a horse who is totally intolerant to having his mane pulled."

Another way to handle the extremely sensitive horse is to braid the entire mane, using the typical three-plait braid (see below), and leave it in for 10 days to 2 weeks. This pulls a lot of the hair out naturally and is a big help in the thinning process."

According to Cindy, a horse's mane doesn't need to pulled every week or two. If you get the mane pulled to the appropriate length, you may not have to do it for a couple months. If you did pull it constantly, the mane would be so thin you wouldn't have anything left by the end of the show season.

Forelock

John and Cindy like to leave the forelock alone. "I think a full forelock is flattering to most horses," John says. "But for a horse with an excessive forelock, I use the clippers and trim the sides of the forelock that spread out toward the ears. I never trim the length or the center of the forelock. I always leave the length alone and just trim the short edges that spread toward the ears. Forelocks are never thinned."

Thinning

Once the mane is pulled to an acceptable length, John uses the thinning shears to complete the thinning and shortening job. He takes his initial cut with the shears where the mane will fall on top of the neck muscle. In other words, he wants the mane to drape on the neck in such a way that when the ends of the hair fall naturally, they lie just above the neck muscle. At this point, there are two layers of hair: the line of hair where John has just cut, and the longer hairs that didn't get trimmed by the thinning shears.

After the initial cut with the shears, John combs out the excess hair before he goes back for a second cut. He makes the second cut about a half-inch below the first cut. By cutting the hair in stages this way, he accomplishes two things. First, it allows him room to work because the hair isn't too short; and second, it helps prevent the blunt-cut look. The goal is to make the ends of the mane look natural and uncut.

"I personally don't like to see a mane that has been banded and then cut off with a pair of regular scissors," says John. "You want to feather the mane and make it look natural."

The second cut leaves a few strands of long hair, making for a three-tiered effect. John cuts the remaining long hairs at an angle, again, so they don't

Once Cindy has pulled the mane to an acceptable length, John starts the thinning process with shears. He takes his initial cut close to where he wants the final mane length to be.

After the first cut with the shears, John combs the mane to remove any loose hair.

This shows the two layers of hair after the initial cut with the shears.

John makes a second cut about a half-inch below the first cut.

There are now three layers of hair—two from the cuts with the shears and the third layer is what's left of the original mane.

John cuts off the long third layer at an angle, so the hair doesn't appear blunt-cut.

John feathers the ends of the mane by undercutting them. He lifts the hairs with the pulling comb and cuts the underlying hairs with the thinning shears.

The next step in the feathering process is to cut through the hair vertically at a slight angle. John does this at half-inch intervals, which further thins and feathers the mane.

appear blunt. However, even with all the pulling, cutting, and thinning, a mane can still look blunt-cut in spots. The next step is to feather the hair.

At this point, John has a fairly good idea of what his length is going to be. He then feathers the ends, starting with the hairs at the horse's withers. He lifts a small section of hair with the pulling comb and then, with the thinning shears, feathers or cuts the hairs under the top layer of hairs he raised. (Beauticians call this undercutting; it's a common practice in cutting human hair.) The length of the mane doesn't change with feathering, but any bluntness the mane might have had starts to disappear. He goes through the mane twice.

Also, by lifting the outside or top hairs during the feathering process, you can see if there are any clumps of thick hair left, or if it's even all the way through. This also tells you where you need to pull the mane more.

Once John has feathered under the mane, he uses the thinning shears to go through the hair vertically at a slight angle, cutting at about half-inch intervals. By using the full length of the shears, he cuts about 2½ inches vertically into the mane. This further thins and feathers the mane.

John can now go back and adjust the mane's length at this point by snipping away any straggling ends. What John ends up with is a nice edge to the mane. The ends of the hairs form a

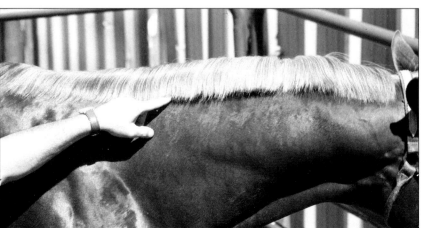

The mane is now starting to take shape. The ends are about the right length and drape over the horse's neck muscle where John wants them.

nice line down the horse's neck, but they are not blunt-cut.

Banding

For pulling, Cindy prefers to work with a dirty mane, but for banding, hair must be clean. She washes and conditions the mane before she bands and likes it to be slightly damp. That makes it easier to work with and as it dries, the banding encourages the hair to lie flat. Cindy bands from the bridle path to the withers.

Cindy starts at the top of the mane and gathers a section of hair about a half-inch wide, using a comb to make her part. On a typical mane, this amount of hair encourages the mane to lie flat after it has been banded. On a real thin mane, she uses more hair for each band. More hair gives the individually banded section more weight. Otherwise, bands on a thin mane tend to make the hair lift up or stick out a little bit.

To separate the rest of the mane from the section she is working on, Cindy uses an alligator clip to hold back the hair.

Cindy holds the section of hair between the forefinger and thumb of her left hand. With the rubber band in her right hand, she wraps around the section of hair, pulling the band to the side every time she makes a wrap. The first two wraps are especially important, she says, and should be tight, so the band holds well. Cindy usually wraps with the band a minimum of four times. For a thick mane, she'll wrap five times around.

With each wrap, the rubber band moves from one hand to the other in a side-to-side motion. Pulling the band in an up-or-down movement, instead of to the side, causes the hair to stick out. The wraps should lie under one another, if possible, and wrapping to the side also helps in achieving this.

Proper wrapping increases the amount of hair actually covered by the band and forces the hair to lie down and flat. Wraps that are jumbled on top of one another produce a knotty effect and look unkempt. It's not always possible to wrap each band neatly 100 percent of the time, but it's worth the effort.

As a final touch after the mane is banded, John returns with the thinning shears and trims any stray or uneven hair in the banded sections.

For horse shows of short duration, say 2 to 3 days, the Weavers keep the bands in the horse's mane, if they'll stay that long. Some bands have to be redone every day because they break loose or the horse rubs them out. But after the show is over, the Weavers take the bands out immediately. Bands tend to break the hair strands and create short hairs that look unsightly.

The easiest way the Weavers have found to remove the bands is by using a seamstress' seam ripper. Simply place the tip of the seam ripper under the band and pull up. That snaps the band and pops it loose without tearing any hair. Rippers are inexpensive and you can find them wherever sewing goods are sold.

Long Manes

There are times when pulling and thinning a mane is not practical, especially if you show in performance classes, like cutting, reining, and roping, where a short, banded mane is not the style. You might want to show the horse in several classes, such as hunt seat and western pleasure, as well as reining. For the pleasure classes, you don't want your horse's mane flying as you lope. That's distracting and you might not catch the judge's eye favorably. One of the techniques mentioned below works well to keep the mane lying still.

There are other reasons to keep a show horse's mane long. Say you want to start a 2-year-old's show career in western pleasure, but you want the horse to rein later on. Reiners, like cutters, are fond of long, flowing manes, and they work long and hard to keep them that way. It seems to enhance the performance in that it gives the illusion of speed and motion. It can take a couple of years for a shortened mane to grow to its original length. Therefore, when showing a pleasure horse who is a reining prospect, it pays to leave the mane alone.

Ropers sometimes use the macrame technique explained below, instead of pulling a mane or roaching it. To them, a mane should not get in the way of the roper's hand or the rope.

After the mane has been washed and conditioned, Cindy bands it. She starts with a half-inch section nearest the bridle path.

Cindy uses the pulling comb to make even parts in the hair and an alligator clip to hold back the hair she isn't working with.

Cindy wraps the band around the section of hair in a side-to-side motion. This encourages the hair to lie flat. Wrapping in an up-and-down motion would encourage the hair to stick up.

Cindy tries to have the wraps lie under one another. That way, the band covers more surface of hair and helps the hair to lie flat. It also looks neater than a band with jumbled-up wraps.

After the hair is banded, John returns with the shears and undercuts the ends of the mane.

As a final touch, he goes through the banded mane vertically with the thinning shears.

Then, too, maybe you don't show horses at all, but want to train an unruly mane to lie on one side of the neck. Using the weight of the mane is one way to accomplish that task.

John and Cindy have never had to thin a long mane. Cindy states: "Usually as the horse grows older, and you wash and comb his mane, it thins itself naturally." However, if a mane is impossibly thick and won't lie down nicely on the horse's neck, it is acceptable to thin it in the same manner explained above; but you will lose some length in the process. Using thinning shears works, but creates a lot of little short hairs sticking out of the long hairs. Cindy's recommendations for extra-thick manes is to really clean and condition them and spray on lots of sheen product. That should keep the hair real soft, so it will lie down, or flow like you want.

Here are two suggestions for handling long manes. The first one, the macrame band, is used most often in show classes. The second one, the three-plait braid, is strictly for training a mane to lie on one side, but it can also be used as an initial effort in pulling a thick mane.

Macrame Band

This technique connects the bands to each other in rows, and the entire mane becomes one unit. The top row of bands doesn't have to be as tightly banded on a long mane as it does on the pulled mane, because the weight of the entire mane helps hold it in place.

First, Cindy separates and bands locks of hair into sections that are about 1½ inches wide. She bands the entire mane and makes an effort to line up the bands carefully. Otherwise, the rows look crooked.

A couple of inches down from the first banded row, she starts the second row. For it and succeeding rows of bands, she combines one half of a banded section with one half of the one next to it. To start, she takes the first band, next to the bridle path, and bands it with half of the second band. Then she takes the remaining half of the second band and combines it with one half of the third band, and so on.

Three-Plait Braid

Braiding the mane is helpful in many areas of hair care. You might want to train a long mane, especially one that falls on both sides of the horse's neck. Or suppose the mane is exceptionally coarse and thick, and you don't relish the thought of the many sessions it

The first step in a macrame pattern is to band the entire mane in sections that are about 1½ inches wide. The bands should be as even as possible.

Starting with the second row and for the succeeding rows of bands, Cindy combines one half of a banded section with one half of the section next to it. This forms the macrame pattern.

A close-up of the pattern.

You can be creative with this pattern. The entire mane can be banded in this manner or only halfway down, allowing the remaining hair to flow freely. It all depends on the effect you are after.

This mane isn't long, but it is thick and unruly. Rather than tackle it with typical pulling and thinning techniques, Cindy braids it, which helps pull out the hair naturally.

For braiding, Cindy divides a 3-inch section of hair into three segments—two outside locks of hair and a middle one. To form a three-plait braid, she takes an outside segment and puts it over the middle one. Then she takes the other outside segment and places it over the new middle segment.

will take to thin it. Or suppose the horse objects to having his mane pulled. In either of the last two situations, braiding adds weight to the hair and pulls some of it out by the roots naturally. The three-plait braid is one way to kill several birds with one stone.

To braid, Cindy divides the hair into sections approximately 3 inches wide. It's easier to braid wet hair than dry, she says, although it doesn't have to be wet or clean. However, wetting the hair might help train it to lie down more quickly.

Each section is further divided into three segments: two outside locks of hair and a middle one. In plaiting, take one outside segment and cross it over the top of the middle segment. Then take the other outside segment and cross it over the new middle segment. This creates a three-plait braid. Cindy braids a section of hair down about three plaits and then wraps a band around the braid to hold it. Then entire mane is done this way. After braiding into three plaits, Cindy lets the rest of the mane fall loose. She says it's not necessary to braid all the way down the mane. "It seems to lift the hair and you don't get as much weight as you do just braiding about three plaits down." She leaves the mane braided for a couple of weeks.

This is also the way Cindy keeps all her horses' manes in the winter, when she wants to keep them trained.

Cindy Weaver's method for wrapping a tail helps to keep it long and full.

Tail Care

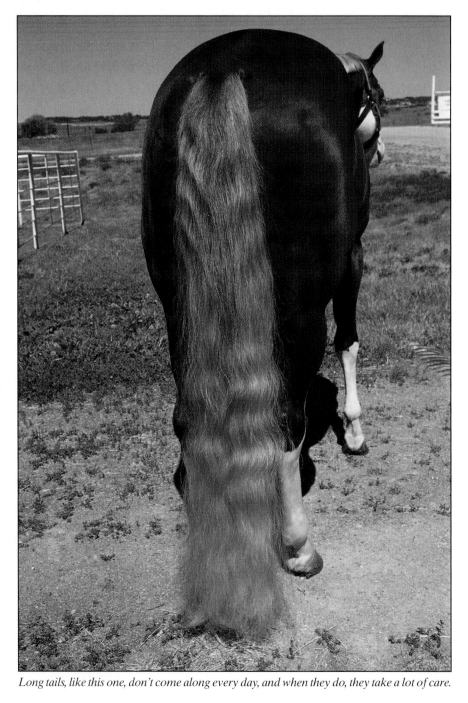

Long tails, like this one, don't come along every day, and when they do, they take a lot of care.

*H*AVING A horse with a long, luxurious tail doesn't happen overnight, if at all. It takes hours of work and dedication to keep a tail from being torn out, stepped on, or rubbed out. A long, full tail, practically dragging the ground, is also a definite plus in the show ring, where it's been the fashion for many years in both English and western classes.

Cindy shows you how she protects horses' tails.

To measure for length, Cindy pulls the tail as far down as it will go.

With a pair of scissors, she cuts the tail hairs even with the ground.

Before You Begin

Tail care begins in the wash rack. How to wash and condition a tail was detailed in Bathing. Dirty tails are usually caked with dirt and grime, making them itchy and tangled—two enemies of a long, abundant tail. A horse will rub a tail that's bothersome, thereby breaking off hairs that take years to grow. Also, the less care a tail receives, the more tangled it gets, and tangles, too, result in hair loss. So Cindy makes sure the tails of the horses in her care are clean, and thoroughly conditioned. She then wraps them to keep them from being exposed to the environment.

Length

For performance horses, other than reiners and ropers, John and Cindy Weaver like the tails to barely touch the ground. But some horses elevate their tails when they are ridden, and the Weavers take that into consideration.

Tails that just barely drag the ground are the ideal for show horses, but few do. And unfortunately for one that does, it must be cut off carefully so the horse won't step on it and rip out hair. To determine where a long tail should be cut off, Cindy holds the tail in one hand and pulls it as far down as it will go. She takes a pair of regular scissors and cuts the tail hairs even with the ground, straight across.

Then she lets the tail go, combs it out, and watches where it lands. With the scissors again, she trims any extra long hairs at the ground line.

In competition, roping and reining horses have to back up and are more susceptible to stepping on their tails. For them, Cindy recommends trimming the tails to the fetlocks. Again, she cuts straight across. That way, the tail is still long and full and she hasn't trimmed away any of the volume.

After trimming the tail, she combs it out, then trims any excess long hair.

Since reining and roping horses are more likely to step on their tails during competition, Cindy trims their tails at the fetlock.

Handy Hint #4

A bed sheet cut into strips forms the tail wrap. A wrap was made out of two sheets—a light-colored sheet and a gold one. The lighter sheet forms the two end strips and the gold one makes up the middle strip. The light strip on the left has been marked with different colored inks to set it apart from the other light strip. This helps show the different sections of hair being braided into the three strips of sheeting.

Many horses lean on their tails during trailering and that wreaks havoc on their tail bone or dock, rubbing out or breaking off strands of hair. To prevent this, wrap the tail bone in an ace bandage. Because it's flexible, an ace bandage usually doesn't restrict the circulation, and it breathes so the horse doesn't sweat underneath it.

John and Cindy don't like to use neoprene tail wraps for extended periods of time because they don't give much. They can get too tight, and it's also possible to forget to take them off right away. On hot days they can cause the horse to sweat, thus starting an irritation around the buttocks or on the tail itself, which can lead to the hair falling out. However, they're fine on short hauls.

Always use caution with any tail wrap, however, If a tail bone is wrapped too tightly, it reduces or eliminates circulation of blood into the tail. This can result in serious injury, and sometimes loss of the tail.

Equipment

Cindy uses a plain bed sheet to wrap her horses' tails. The size of the sheet makes no difference—either twin, double, queen, or king. They are all about the same length and it's the length that's important in wrapping the tail using this method. The sheet needs to be long enough to encompass the entire tail.

She cuts or tears the sheet lengthwise into two 6-inch-wide strips. She folds one of the strips in half and tears it down the middle. Now she has one long continuous piece and one half of a long continuous piece, which will make up the three streamers of her tail wrap as explained below.

To assemble the tail wrap out of the two strips, she lays the long continuous piece horizontally on the ground. In the middle of this piece she places the short piece vertically, forming a T.

Cindy doesn't knot the two pieces together to form one unit, even though it appears that would be the logical step. "Just laying the short piece down in the middle of the long piece is the secret of this wrap," Cindy says. "If you tie the two pieces into a knot, as some people do, then you have a knot that sits at the base of the tail bone, where all the long hair grows from. When the horse swishes his tail, the knot is extra weight and helps to pull the long hairs out."

Wrapping

Cindy then places the center of the newly formed tail wrap under and around the tail about an inch below the bottom of the tail bone. This is where she divides the tail into three sections of hair and starts braiding. The braiding is similar to the three-plait

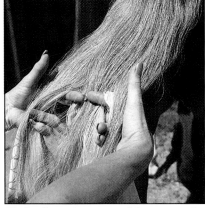

Cindy places the center of the wrap under and around the tail about an inch below the bottom of the tail bone. She divides the tail into three sections of hair, each with its own strip of wrapping.

Cindy begins a three-plait braid. She starts with the right-hand light strip and places it over the middle gold strip. This photo shows her placing the left-hand light strip (with ink stripe pattern) over the plain light strip, which is now the middle section.

This close-up of the wrap shows how each strip of sheeting encloses the section of hair. Notice how no hair is exposed to the environment.

Cindy continues braiding all the way down the tail. There should be about 6 inches of sheeting left over.

Cindy ties a half-hitch with the leftover strip, and . . .

. . . pulls it through the braid tightly.

braid explained in Mane Care.

She gathers the right strip of sheeting along with the right section of hair and the left strip with the left section of hair. The center strip and section of hair just hang down the middle. She supports this section with her three middle fingers. Now she starts braiding with the three pieces. She crosses the right strip of sheeting (which has the right section of tail enclosed) over the middle one. That forms a new middle section. Then she takes the left strip of sheeting (which encloses the left section of hair) and places it over the middle one in a typical three-plait braid. She pulls each braid tight as she goes, especially the top few braids. As she braids, she carefully encloses all of the tail hairs in the sheeting, so they are not exposed at all.

When she has braided all of the tail, Cindy ties off the leftover sheeting.

"Ideally," she explains, "you'd like to have 6 or more inches left over when you've completed your braid. The longer your sheet can be past the tail, the better."

To tie off the wrapped braid, Cindy makes a half-hitch with the longest of the leftover sections, pulling it tight.

In summertime, you can let the leftover tail wrap hang down so the horse can still swat flies with it. Or you can tie pieces of twine in the end to act as a fly swatter. In winter, Cindy usually ties it off in a knot. This keeps it out of the dirt.

Cindy keeps all of her horses' tails in this configuration until show time. However, she only leaves the wrap in for 2 weeks at a time. Then she removes the wrap and rewraps the hair. She says if the hair above the wrap ever looks ratted or knotted, you have to take the wrap off immediately and redo it. In the summer, she takes the wraps off the tail once a

A completed and tied off braid.

Handy Hint #5

Horses rub their tails for several reasons. Even if their tails are clean, some horses rub them due to boredom, habit, or pinworms. That can cause rashes and scabs, which, in turn, cause the horse to rub more. Keeping a horse busy and exercised might help. If a horse is suffering from pinworms, ask your veterinarians for a dewormer that will treat that type of worm.

Also, a mare can have a dirt buildup in the udder or vulva areas that causes her to itch. In an effort to alleviate that itch, she will rub her tail. If that problem exists, frequent cleansing should help the problem.

Cindy has tied pieces of baling twine in the end of the tail wrap. This helps the horse to swat flies in the summer.

Cindy likes to use tail bags at shows. She'll often use both a sheet wrap and a tail bag to completely enclose a tail.

week, combs the hair out, and then wraps it again. In the winter, she feels she can leave the wrap in for about a month at a time. In the summer, it's more crucial to watch for hair being pulled out because the horse is so active swishing flies.

Because each section of hair is encased in a sheet, the hair stays clean and you have less breakage.

Tail Bag

Braiding the hair and putting it in a tail bag is great for going to a show, Cindy says. She likes the bags with the VELCRO® closure at the top because VELCRO doesn't seem to pull the hair as badly and the bags stay on better. But for long-term use, Cindy says you end up breaking hair in a tail bag because the braids will cause friction when they rub against one another.

Cindy doesn't like to use socks as tail bags. It's a common practice, but you have to tie a knot to keep a sock in place on the tail and every time you have a knot, Cindy says, you run the risk of breaking off and pulling out hairs.

Cindy uses waterproofed tail bags, especially on mares. When a mare urinates, she can soak the sheet tail wrap. Urine can damage and burn a tail. So Cindy puts a waterproofed tail bag over the sheet tail wrap and that keeps the hair dry. It's just another layer of protection for the tail hair.

One word of caution: Keeping a tail braided and wrapped might not be wise on a horse kept in a corral or pasture, as he might snag it on something and rip out a bunch of hair.

Handy Hint #6

When your horse's tail is not in a braid or tail bag, you can keep it off the ground while riding by tying half-hitch knots in three or four large sections of hair. Tie the knots up high in the tail. That raises the length of the tail just enough so the horse won't step on it if he backs up. This is perfect for schooling during horse shows because the horse won't step on it when you warm him up before a class.

John and Cindy Weaver show you how they get a horse ready just before they step into the arena.

Show Time

A lot goes into presenting a pretty picture for the judge. Here, John shows the yearling Filly N Swiss, owned by Robin Ehlers, Kiowa, Colo., to the reserve grand champion mare title.

*A*FTER ALL the clipping, bathing, trimming, banding, and braiding, it's show time for John and Cindy and their horses. All their hard work pays off when one of their horses enters the arena and exits with a ribbon.

We'll go through the routine the Weavers have perfected to get their horses ready for the show arena.

Before and after. Above, 3-year-old Red Hot Sonny had just come from wintering in west Texas. He's underweight, rough-coated, and out of shape. Below, after 90 days of care by the Weavers, he is slick, in good shape, and ready for the show ring. The stallion is owned by George Pachelo of Denver.

DAY BEFORE THE SHOW

There are several things John and Cindy do the day before the show that help immensely once they're there. Here's a rundown of their grooming process.

Vacuuming

Cindy vacuums as much dirt and dust as possible before she washes the horse. "I start at the neck and go over the entire body, even the mane and tail," she explains. "Vacuuming brings up a lot of dead hair that would be hard to get out any other way."

"We're fortunate to have hot water and a heated barn," says John. "However, in the winter, if you didn't have those facilities, and few people do, you'd have to use the vacuum because you couldn't wash your horse in a cold barn. We also use the vacuum between baths. There are times when bathing a horse is inconvenient, and vacuuming is handier and more simple."

"Also," Cindy exclaims, "vacuuming helps bring up the oil in the horse's skin, and that helps the haircoat look

John and Cindy use their handy-dandy Vac 'N Blo at home as well as at shows. Vacuuming is one of the best ways to pick up loose dirt and hair. Also, it's perfect when the weather is too cold to give a horse a bath.

healthy and shiny.

"Also, I use the vacuum before and after I exercise a horse, either by longeing or riding," Cindy continues. "But if he gets sweaty, then I rinse him."

When Cindy vacuums a horse's legs, she uses the brush attachments instead of the regular, triangular suction attachment. The latter doesn't conform easily to the bone and tendon areas. And besides it's usually made of hard plastic, which would not be comfortable to a horse.

"There are several kinds of brush attachments to use, and I even use them on the horse's face," Cindy says.

Washing

They wash their horses at the barn before they go to the show. "When you're in a familiar place," John says, "there's less confusion. Sometimes we have to bathe the horses at the show grounds, but we try to get it done beforehand."

Manes and Tails

Cindy bands the manes of horses who won't rub them out. Those who will rub are banded at the show grounds or the morning of the class. Tails are washed, conditioned, and braided, but without the sheet wraps that were explained and illustrated in Tail Care. Tails are simply braided into a three-plait braid and put into a nylon tail bag.

Leg Wraps

Horses' legs are wrapped for the trailer ride and, if it's a weekend show, they stay on overnight to help keep legs clean.

Supplies

The Weavers make sure that supplies, such as hay, grain, tack, buckets, and grooming equipment, are loaded in the trailer. And they pack a first-aid kit, as well as necessities such as clippers, fly spray, coat conditioner, etc.

Once they arrive at the show grounds, John and Cindy check the stall conditions. If the floors are dusty, they wet them down with a hose before bedding the stalls with shavings. This helps to keep the horses from breathing dusty air, which can cause lung congestion. And it helps prevent the dust from settling on the horses' haircoats.

The Weavers bed deeply enough so the horses don't scratch their legs getting up and down. Then, they unload them from the trailer and put them into the freshly bedded stalls.

Water buckets are hung next. During the summertime, the Weavers hang two water buckets so horses have enough water. In cool weather, one bucket is generally enough.

DAY OF THE SHOW

Here's a summary of what the Weavers do on the day of the show. A more detailed account of each step in the grooming process follows.

First, they feed the horses and clean stalls. As the horses are finishing their feed, the Weavers take them out one at a time and prepare them for the day.

They remove the horse's sheet, hood, leg wraps, and tail bag. They comb out the tail and Cindy rebraids it if necessary. Then John applies hoof black and razors the horse's nose. Once the hoof black dries, they put that horse back in his stall until just before the class, when he'll get a final grooming.

When it gets closer to class time, the horse is tied in the stall and vacuumed, or thoroughly groomed with brushes. They take the horse out of the stall and spray him with coat conditioner and fly spray, if necessary, and Cindy puts highlighter on the face. Then the horse is tied back in the stall with a cooler on.

If the Weavers have many youth or amateur exhibitors going at one time, which is often the case in showmanship classes, John usually stations himself at the arena for any last-minute grooming. Cindy stays back at the stalls getting horses ready and sending them to the arena with their owners.

After the horse is finished with a class, he goes back to his stall and on go his sheet and hood to keep him clean. However, in really hot weather, the Weavers may elect to leave the clothing off. Both the halter horses and the performance horses are rinsed in the evening. Then they are dressed again with sheet, hood, tail bag, and leg wraps until the next day.

Here's a more detailed account of the grooming process.

Washing

Even though a horse was washed the day before the show, it's possible for him to get manure stains on white legs or body markings. To help prevent staining, the Weavers use leg wraps, sheets, and hoods as a barrier against the environment.

There's usually no time for another bath, so John and Cindy use emergency measures to get the horse clean. If the spot is a fresh manure stain, the Weavers try rubbing it out with a rubber curry comb and a stiff brush. Then

Cindy dips a chamois cloth in water, squeezes it out, and wets the area. "The chamois absorbs some of the stain," Cindy says, "but it will still look dirty until the hair dries.

"The sheen product we spray on after the horse's bath helps repel stains. Because it doesn't allow a stain to sink in totally, we can wash it away."

It's important to keep stalls clean, not only at home, but at shows. This lessens the chance of manure stains. During the show, the Weavers clean stalls several times a day, and that also helps keep the flies away.

Vacuuming

John says, "If you can't bathe a dirty horse because of cool weather, wash the legs and then vacuum the body. Vacuuming doesn't take long and it really sucks up dirt and dust."

For a riding horse who gets sweaty under the saddle, Cindy recommends wiping the sweat with a cloth, and then vacuuming the horse when he dries.

Vacuuming is one of the last things John and Cindy do before they tie a horse in his stall to wait for a class.

Horse Clothing

To protect horses from the weather and to keep haircoats, manes, and tails from dust and dirt, the Weavers use sheets, hoods, and tail bags. They're also good for protecting horses from flies. If it is cold, the horses also wear winter blankets and hoods.

John and Cindy prefer nylon sheets over cotton. They say cotton tends to pull the hair and make it lie unevenly; whereas, nylon keeps the coat shiny and smooth. The Weavers also use nylon tail bags, with VELCRO® clo-

sures, to protect braided tails from dirt and urine.

They leave the sheets, hoods, and tail bags on the horses all night, and remove them in the morning for grooming. Once a horse has gone through the entire grooming process, then John and Cindy tie him in his stall and put on a nylon cooler. The cooler is handy for several reasons. It helps keep the dust off the horse's coat and can be taken off rapidly. Depending on where the horse's stall is in relation to the arena, the horse might wear the cooler until just minutes before the class.

Leg Wraps

"Some people swear by leg wraps and some swear at them," states John. The Weavers wrap mainly for support in hauling and for cleanliness in the stalls.

Even if the Weavers haul horses a short distance, they wrap their legs, at least the front ones, with quilts and nylon bandages. They don't like the type of quilt that has a diamond-shaped pattern to the stitching, however, since pressure points can affect circulation in the horse's legs.

"I recommend two types of quilts," Cindy offers. "One is a synthetic fleece, offered in some of the equine supply catalogs. Or you can buy the material at a fabric shop (a coat lining fleece) and make your own. Cut the fleece 15 inches wide and 30 inches long. However, I think the fleece quilts found in catalogs are a little bigger. Fleece doesn't bind or cause any pressure points on the horse's legs. The fabric also breathes enough not to trap too much heat."

Another advantage to the synthetic

The Weavers prefer to use nylon sheets and hoods.

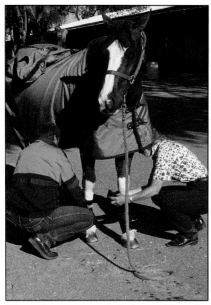

They always wrap their horses' legs for support while trailering and to prevent manure staining while in the stalls.

Two kinds of leg quilts. On the left is a short, foam-lined cotton wrap. On the right is a longer, synthetic fleece quilt. Both are wrapped with nylon leg bandages.

fleece is its ability to be washed repeatedly. The Weavers wash their quilts often because of the large number of horses they must deal with.

To secure the fleece quilt, Cindy uses a nylon bandage, as opposed to the traditional cotton variety. "The cotton ones are too short," explains Cindy, "and as you pull them tight, they tend to bunch up."

The nylon bandage they like has a VELCRO® fastener and is relatively new to the market. It doesn't bunch and it stretches enough so circulation is not cut off.

The other quilt Cindy recommends is a foam-lined, cotton wrap, which can be found in tack stores. Cindy thinks they are a little short in width, but still work well. "They do give good support and, again, you can't bunch them up to the point where you cut off circulation."

The Weavers wrap the cannon bone from just below the knee or hock to just below the fetlock joint. This protects the tendons and ligaments running alongside the cannon bones. With the longer synthetic fleece quilts there is leftover quilt material on both ends, which lends some protection to the knee or hock and pastern.

Cindy places the quilt midway on the inside of the cannon bone and wraps in a clockwise direction. Then, using the same wrapping pattern, she circles the quilt with the nylon bandage. Again, she starts midway on the inside of the cannon bone and wraps around and down the leg. Once she gets to the fetlock she goes back up again and finishes just below the knee (or hock on the hind leg). The VELCRO® fastener secures the wrap.

The Weavers have found that some

To wrap, Cindy starts midway on the inside of the cannon bone and wraps clockwise.

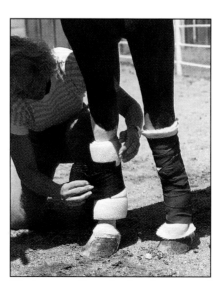

Cindy wraps the nylon bandage around the quilt in the same clockwise direction.

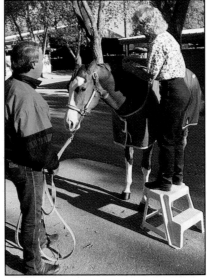

If the bands in a horse's mane have fallen out or become ragged-looking, Cindy bands them again.

horses do not like wraps around the bottom of their fetlocks, especially on the hind legs. Evidently, they find them uncomfortable and often kick trying to get them off. So, with those horses, the Weavers use the shorter, foam-lined cotton wraps and just wrap the cannon bone area.

Manes and Tails

After they remove a horse's hood, John and Cindy take a good look at the mane. If it needs rebanding or a touch-up trim, they redo what needs to be done.

They remove the tail bag and comb out the tail for the initial grooming. If there's time before the class, Cindy might rebraid the tail and put it back into the tail bag until final grooming before the class. Right before the horse goes into the arena, the tail bag

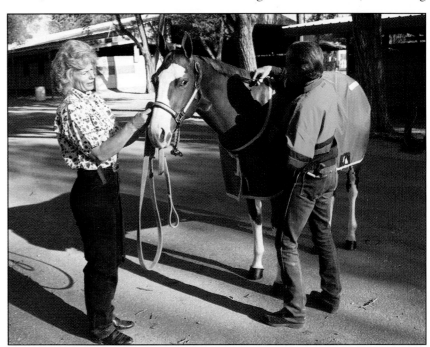

John gives a mane a last-minute touch-up trim.

After John removes the tail bag, Cindy unbraids the tail, combs it out, and sprays on a sheen product.

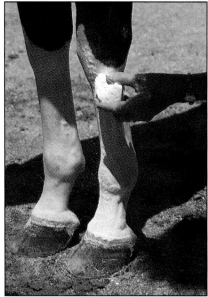

With French White, Cindy chalks a horse's white legs.

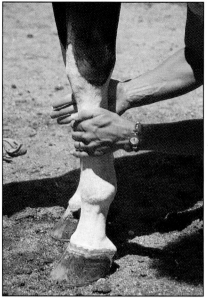

Cindy rubs the chalk into the horse's leg to make it adhere better.

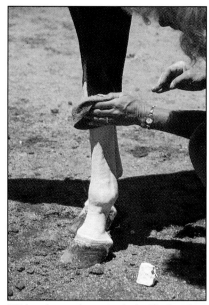

With a damp chamois cloth, Cindy wipes away excess chalk from the horse's dark hair.

comes off and the tail is combed and sprayed with conditioner (a sheen product). If for some reason the top of the tail is bushy, it's wrapped with a bandage (such as an Ace bandage or a leg wrap) before the class to help it lie down.

After the class, the tail is rebraided and put back into a tail bag.

Chalking the Legs

To make white legs brighter and whiter, Cindy uses either chalk or baby powder mixed with corn starch. She mixes the baby powder and corn starch 50-50 and applies it with a powder puff. After the horse is thoroughly dusted, she rubs the white powder in with her hands to blend it and make it adhere to the horse's skin. Then she cleans any excess off the horse's hoofs, because John polishes them with hoof black.

Even though this method is easiest to use, Cindy prefers using chalk. Horse's legs must be clipped short for the chalk to adhere. If the hair is a little long, then the baby powder-corn starch method must be used. The chalk, called French White, is actually a grooming product for dogs and cats. There is nothing comparable in the equine market. Cindy gets it at dog shows or orders it out of pet product catalogs.

The chalk comes in block form and Cindy rubs it up and down the horse's leg, as if she were writing on a chalk board. She works in long strokes, from the coronet band up. The chalk adheres to the leg easily and blends in well. Cindy rubs it past the white leg hair and into the dark hair, so there is no line of demarcation between the two. Then, she runs a damp cloth or chamois down the leg, quickly and lightly, removing the chalk from the dark hair and leaving the leg looking natural. The chalk can be used on face markings, as well.

Cindy also likes the chalk because it seems to repel dust and dirt better. "I can chalk my pleasure horses," she explains, "and their legs still look good by the end of the day."

Hoof Black

John tries to use a new bottle of hoof black at every show because the applicator sponge is in good shape to apply the liquid in a smooth, straight line. After the bottle is used several times, the applicator gets a ragged edge to it and isn't as accurate.

Getting a new bottle of hoof black for every show might not be practical for the single-horse owner. Therefore, John recommends watching the condition of the applicator sponge.

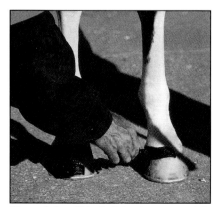

To apply hoof black, John draws a straight line across the top of the hoof and then fills in the rest.

When it gets torn, he suggests getting a new bottle.

To apply hoof black, John makes one smooth line around the top of the hoof, even with the coronet band, and then fills in the rest of the hoof.

If the show goes for several days, John applies fresh hoof black each day. For horses who show in both halter and performance, he may even reapply hoof black before the performance classes, especially if it's a major show. He likes to use the type of hoof black that washes off easily.

Razoring the Nose

John uses a disposable razor to shave the stubble on a horse's nose. Clippers, with the number 40 blades, do a good job of removing most of a horse's whiskers, but still leave short, stubbly hairs. It's like a 5 o'clock shadow on a man's face. Because the disposable variety shaves closely, there is a chance of nicking the horse's skin, so John is careful. He razors all around the nose, inside the nostrils, and under the lower lip.

John uses a disposable razor to clean up the short, stubbly hairs on a horse's nose, nostrils, and lips.

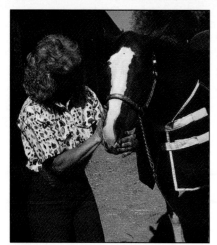

Cindy uses face highlighter on the eyelids and muzzle.

Face Highlighters

Cindy oils the eyelids and muzzle with one of several products on the market designed to highlight the horse's face. Some people use baby oil, but Cindy does not. It can cause a horse's nose to blister, especially if the skin is pink. The oil also makes the nose look even pinker.

Face highlighters come in three colors: black, white, and clear. For horses with pink noses, Cindy uses white so she can blend it into the skin to tone down the pink color. Yet, she says, the horse still looks natural.

Some of the face highlighters come with sunscreen to help protect the horse from ultraviolet rays. Even though Cindy uses this type, she still applies sunscreen formulated for humans, with the sun protection value of 30. She rubs it over the muzzle and eyelids before she applies highlighter. She is careful not to let it drip into the horse's eyes. Baby oil is prone to dripping, but the horse product is more stable.

Cindy uses a fly repellent on horses' ears. It not only keeps out the bugs, it also helps to put a shine on ears. After wiping the ears inside and out with a damp chamois cloth, she puts the repellent either on her hands or on a rag and wipes the ears again, as well as the entire poll area.

Cindy does not use petroleum jelly as a highlighter, because it collects dirt.

Coat Conditioner

Cindy sprays the horse's body, mane, and tail with a coat conditioner designed to make hair shine and to untangle manes and tails. "It's oily and does collect some dust," she admits, "so I'm careful when I use it. Sometimes I don't use it the first day of a show because the horses are really clean and shiny. But, by the second

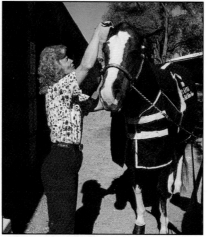

With a damp chamois cloth, Cindy cleans out a horse's ears and then applies fly repellent with her hands or a rag.

day, they've collected some dust and dirt, and their coats, manes, and tails are a little dull. So I spray them before they go into the arena to help bring back the highlights."

After spraying she wipes the horse with a towel or uses a soft brush. She tries not to spray the saddle area because some conditioners make the hair so slippery the saddle will not stay positioned correctly.

In-Gate

Unless the Weavers are running late for a class, the horse goes to the arena with the cooler on. John always brings a comb, soft brush, towel, damp chamois, and fly spray (during fly season) to the in-gate for last-minute grooming.

He removes the cooler and sprays the horse once more lightly over the

body, but more on the legs and the belly where flies land frequently. John suggests a light spray because too much causes wet spots. Besides looking unsightly, the wet hair can stand up in the sun and also pick up more dirt. John then brushes the horse all over and towels out the nose if it looks dirty.

The clean, well-turned-out horse is now ready for the show ring. John and Cindy have done their jobs in presenting the animal to his best advantage.

John and Cindy Weaver have shown how they pay attention to details, and it's the details that make all the difference when it comes to grooming and caring for your horse. The Weavers have offered the tips and tricks of the trade, whether you want to show your horse or just know how to make him look his best.

At the in-gate, the Weavers give a horse a last-minute once-over.